TEARS
OF A
MANN

Poetic Chronicles Of A Young Heart

DANIEL E. BETHEA, JR.

Lightning Fast Book Publishing, LLC
P.O. Box 441328
Fort Washington, MD 20744

www.lfbookpublishing.com

All rights reserved. No part of this book may be reproduced or transmitted in any form or by any means—electronic, mechanical, photocopying, recording, or otherwise—without written permission from the author, except for the inclusion of brief quotations in a review.

The author of this book provides a poetic chronicle of his life experiences. The intent is to take readers through his emotional life journey. In the event that you use or enact any of the material in this book, the author and publisher assume no responsibility for your actions.

The publisher, Lightning Fast Book Publishing, assumes no responsibility for any content presented in this book.

Copyright © 2017
Daniel E. Bethea, Jr.
All rights reserved.

Library of Congress Control Number: 2013903051
ISBN-10: 0-9974925-7-0
ISBN-13: 978-0-9974925-7-6

CONTENTS

A Dance In Romance

4 Seasons 9
A Fountain 10
A Search of the Heart 11
A Song of Solomon 12
A Thought 14
A Treasure Untold. 15
A Tribute to My Girl 16
An Offer. 17
Black Butterfly 18
Blessed 19
Butterflies. 20
Dear Love. 21
Enchanting Waters 22
Essence of Love 23
Extend Your Hand 24
Holiness 25
How Can I Express These Feelings 27
Image of Beauty 28
Kiss of Dawn 29
Lay Back. 30
Let Me 31
Love? 32
Love Eternal. 34
Love Psalm. 35
Man Without Woman 36
Mesmerized 37
Motion of Stillness. 38
My Dreams, Visions, and Hallucinations 40
My Queen 42
Mystical Desire. 43

Precious 45
Simple Thoughts 46
Smile 47
The Question.. 48
These Feelings 49
Thirst for Love.. 51
Total Eclipse... 52
True Essence 53
Your Beauty... 54
Your Fragrance 55

Tears of a Mann

A Novel of Mystery 59
An Expression of Pain 61
Can We Talk?... 62
Days go by 64
Every Time... 66
Hey Babe 67
I Blew It! 68
Love Experience.. 72
Silence 74
Tears Of A Mann 75
Tired... 77
The Question—The Answer 78

A Walk In the Spirit

A Battle 83
A Message 85
A Simple Favor.. 87
A Talk with Satan....................................... 89
After the Storm 91
Ashamed... 92
Comforter.. 94
Curiosity... 95
Examination of Myself................................. 96

Focus	97
Heavy Heart	98
How?	100
It's yours to Control	101
My Lord Speaks	102
My Understanding	103
Perspective	105
Razor Sharp Imagination	107
Realization	108
Reflection	110
The Choice	112
The Roads of Life	113
Total Understanding	114
What Type of Love is This?	115
Who's Army	117
Why?	119
Wondering	120
Your Choice	121
About the Author	123

A DANCE IN ROMANCE

Sweet dreams
Of Crackling candlelight

Reflections of crystal
Moonlight

Essence of Love
Dancing in Romance

Seasons change
But Romance is forever

4 SEASONS

Mellow streams,
Whispering dawns,
Silent breeze,
Quiet storms,
All these beautiful things
I find within you.

I look into your eyes and
I tend not to be surprised,
For within you there lies
A world filled with four different seasons;
Giving off the essence of your great wonders.

All year round
I watch rivers form into oceans;
Oceans of great love.
I see soft gentle mist
Turn into great thunderstorms;
Thunderstorms of raging passion.

As the leaves fall to the ground,
I fall to my knees in the presence of your pounding heart
Knowing a queen has entered my presence,
And like royalty shall I treat her.

A FOUNTAIN

As I dip my cup into your fountain
I draw up more than the fresh taste of water.

I draw up the flavor of sweet juices
Sweetened just right
To quench my thirst for your love.

I draw up the essence of a field of roses
In full bloom to capture
The moments of our passion.

I draw up a meal
That is powerful enough to calm
The craving for your sensual touch.

I draw up a vessel of oil Filled with the fragrance Of your tasteful body.

When I dip my cup into your fountain
I draw up more than the fresh taste of water.
I draw up the love for your inner soul.

A SEARCH OF THE HEART

As I look into your eyes
I realize my search is over
I've searched God's great earth For someone as special as you
And found no one.

I searched the heavens
And found not one shining star.
I searched the depths of the ocean
And found not one beautiful pearl.

I searched the lowest of valleys
And found not a spring of water.
I searched the highest of mountains
And found not my treasure of virtue.

But with the soft touch of your hand
You placed my heart at ease,
Completing its journey in search
Of that perfect love.

No longer will my heart search
For a lover to fill this empty void
Within my heart.

A SONG OF SOLOMON

Deep inside
My passion for you
Flows like an endless stream;
My love for you
Is like an endless dream.

I think about you
Night and day,
Allowing this path of love
To take me where it may.

How I long to see your face
How I long to feel your embrace

Your soft kisses
Are like a gentle breeze
Caressing my lips
With the greatest of ease.

You send my heart on a voyage
Searching out the depth of our love.
Knowing no one can understand
Except for he that lies above.

Your warm embrace,
That undefiled smile
You have upon your face.

How can a man contain the love that you give?
So warm, so sweet and supple.
It makes me want to live.

"O my dove, that art in the clefts of the rock,
in the secret places of the stairs,
Let me see thy face; let me hear thy voice.
For sweet is thy voice, and thy face is beautiful."

Song 2:14

A THOUGHT

I look in the mirror and I see a vision of loveliness.
I say, If I could be anyone else in the world, I would still be me.
My life has not been without mistakes, but then whose has?
I am by no means perfect, but who is?
I realize I am a unique individual, for I know things that others do not know;
I do things others cannot do;
I feel things others may not or cannot feel;
And I see things others cannot see;
Knowing these things, I realize I am intelligent.
I am glad that I am me.
I know that I touch lives because I am thought about.
I am thought of and I am remembered, therefore, I am more than nothing.
I am a part of lives and a valuable part of life.
I am a bottle of fine champagne that is to be sipped not gulped.
I am to be savored, not discarded.
I am a valued piece of merchandise that is to be handled gently and carefully.
I am to love and be loved.
I am to be surrounded with positively beautiful things because
I am a part of God's creation and
I AM BEAUTIFUL.

Just a thought

A TREASURE UNTOLD

Your tears are priceless,
Your smiles are worth more than gold,
Your eyes sparkle like diamonds,
You are a treasure untold.

Your kiss is more pleasurable than a gentle breeze;
Your touch softer than a rose petal;
Oh how it sets my heart at ease.

You are a ray of beauty that brings forth
The color in roses.
You are the essence of flowers,
That brings forth life in my soul.

If no one ever told you,
You're a treasure untold.

A TRIBUTE TO MY GIRL . . .

The beauty that you posses,
No man's eyes can contain.
The love that you give,
No man's heart can hold.
You are like unto the moon,
Shinning so bright through the darkness.
You shine and show your ability to comfort,
And love when I am in need.
You hold and caress me
Until all is right.
You stay by my side through thick and thin,
Making sure I don't stumble and fall.
The kisses of your soft lips
Are more than I can handle.
Those kisses let me know you care,
Not a little, but a great deal.
Without you in my life,
I know not what to do.
You were there in my time of joy,
In my time of sadness.
In my time of wealth.
In my time of need.
You are more than a lover.
You are more than a comforter.
You are more than what I need.
For you I give you nothing less than
The full love of my heart,
For you are my one and only true love,
My one and only true girlfriend,
My mother.
I love you Ma . . .

AN OFFER

I'll give you
Emeralds,
Diamonds,
Pearls.
I'll even give you the world if I must.
Just to gain your trust,
I'll even eat your dust.

I just want to be loved by you.
Hugged by you,
Kissed by you,
Missed by you.

Why,
Because you are more beautiful to me,
Than moonlight.
Sweeter than
The nectar of a dozen roses.

They say love comes and goes,
But the memories we can hold
Like solid gold.

You see,
This can be,
Only if you choose not to be lonely.

BLACK BUTTERFLY

Beautiful and black are ye,
To a butterfly must I compare thee.

Gracefully flying,
Dancing with its many stripes and colors,
Beautiful is the essence of this
Beautiful black butterfly.

In your eyes I see,
The mysteries of never-ending stories.

I see my shining star,
My morning dew.

And it is to you
I do give my heart to,
For you are my
Beautiful Black Butterfly.

BLESSED

As I feel the sun's rays caressing my face,
Giving me warmth throughout my body,
I think of your love
Warming up my cold and damp heart.

You placed your loving arms around me,
Gently caressing my inner spirit,
Touching me in places I've never been touched before,
Filling the empty voids I never could fill.

With your light shining so bright,
I can clearly see the way.
Throughout my day,
Those dark clouds tend to roll away,
And I have no one to thank but "You Lord."

I love you.

BUTTERFLIES

I get butterflies in my stomach
When you walk into my room.
I begin to hallucinate and fantasize
About these feelings which I hide.

You see,
My dreams are slowly becoming a reality.

I want to travel to worlds never discovered,
I want to take a journey though the stars,
And stop on that planet of love.

For your love is like a dove;
Pure, innocent and white.
It's an image of beauty,
Manifested through God's great nature.

I want you to bless me with your rays of beauty.
Knock me to my knees.
Have me begging you please,
"Shine your light on me."

I want you to be mine
Until the end of time.

DEAR LOVE

My love,

Even though we are far apart,
I leave you a key to my heart.
You can come when you may
I just ask that you don't delay.

You see,
My heart burns with a fire
Strong enough to consume your every desire.
My feelings run deeper than any ocean or sea.
I just ask that you take a chance with me.

Open your eyes and realize
I have dreams and fantasies.
Wanting so badly for them to become reality
But only you hold the key to unlock this fantasy.

I ask that you keep in mind,
When you sit down to unwind,
These feelings I have inside.

ENCHANTING WATERS

To see you smile
Is to compare you to a dozen sunsets.
You are as beautiful as moonlight
Caressing the ocean's naked waves.

Look deep into my eyes and see
That there is a river forming,
An ocean of great capacity;
An ocean of great love.

If you wish to experience a
Love greater than you can ever imagine,
Greater than you can ever handle,

Take a dip into my ocean
And become drenched by the waters
Of my love.

ESSENCE OF LOVE

Not even a garden of roses
Can match the essence you give off,

For your beauty is more
Than breathtaking.

Not even a picture can
Capture the beauty you posses.

Making love to you
Is not even on my mind,
For I want to show you
My dreams until the end of time.

I want to walk down
This path of love;
Making it pure, white and innocent
Like unto a beautiful dove,
Without any spots of blemishes.

I want to travel
To distant lands
Hand in hand
Walking on jet black sand.

Understand,
I want to love you for life,
For this is the reason why I live.

EXTEND YOUR HAND

What if I told you I want to love you for life?
Would you extend your hand and give me a chance?

What if I told you I promise to hold you tight,
On those cold lonely nights;
Be your laughter when things aren't right;
Be your comforter when things go wrong.

Would you take a chance as I extend my hand?

I'll be your company on those lonely nights.
I'll be there with you till all is right.
I'll be your joy when you are sad.
I'll help face your anger when you are mad.

I am willing to be your man;
All I ask for is a chance.
If I told you I love you,
Would you extend your hand?

HOLINESS

As I look into your eyes
I see the sun,
The moon,
The stars,
And the Holy heavens.

I see rivers of love,
Oceans of emotions,
And waterfalls of great passion.

I have become stunned by your beauty
Which God has blessed you with.

To watch you is like
Watching a flower bloom in the spring.

To feel the touch of your hand
Is to feel the soft touch of rose petals
Caressing my face.

For me to stand by your side,
I feel honored.

I will bless the Lord
For the rest of my days,
For giving me someone so special as you.

I can say so many words
To express the way I want you,
But I will sum it up
In three simple words:

I love you.

HOW CAN I EXPRESS THESE FEELINGS

How can I express
How much I miss you?
There are not enough words
To express these emotions I feel.

Missing you is like
Living in a world void and without form.
It's like living in a world of confusion;
Caught up in a mist of illusions.

Missing the sweet sound of your voice
Piercing the night sky.
Missing the soft touch of your gentle lips,
Captivating my every emotion.
Missing the taste of your chocolate hips,
Quenching my hunger for your love.
Missing your hands caressing my chest,
Sending my heart cruising into eternal love.

Missing you is like losing a part of me.
I shall not rest until I find my other half.
I will not rest until you are in my loving arms at last.

IMAGE OF BEAUTY

You're a piece of art,
Men consider as a masterpiece.

You're a butterfly
Splashed with the color of virtue.

You're a river of love
Flowing in my heart.

For you to lay in my arms
And watch the sunset,
It sends my heart on a voyage,
Searching for the depth and meaning of your love.

As I sleep,
I feel the touch of your gentle hands,
Caressing my face.

I traveled a thousand seas
And landed on your sand.
To contemplate my next journey
And make my plans.

I ask you,
Are you ready
To spend your life
In my arms in Paradise?

KISS OF DAWN

Like the kiss of Dawn,
Allow me to awaken a beautiful flower
With a gentle kiss.

I want to awaken
That flower that has the power
To devour the pain and agony
Of a broken heart.

I want to awaken
That flower that will
Mend this broken vessel
And fill it with its pure love.

I want that flower to be
My earth, my sun,
My moon, my stars;
I want that flower to be my galaxy
That will stand next to me.

For I want this flower to be a lady
But first . . .
Allow me to awaken a beautiful flower
With a gentle kiss.

LAY BACK

Lay on your back and close your eyes.
Allow me to lie by your side.

Let me explore the caverns of your heart.
Let my sense of adventure run wild within.

Jump into my sea of pleasure
To experience all your dreams and fantasies.

You see,
Deep within lies a river,
Flowing with the purity of my love.

If you look a little deeper,
You will find a burning inferno,
Blazing with the greatness of my passion.

So allow me to give
You the tender embrace
Of a gentle rose.

Kisses like a gentle mist.
Touches soft as a silent breeze.

Hear my heart pound
With the sound of
A great waterfall.

Allow me to
Journey into the depths of your heart,
Finding the hidden treasures of your love.

LET ME

Let me fall six feet in love with you.
I don't have to step into your love,
I'm willing to jump into this endless well of love.
But only if you allow me to.

Allow me to spark this fire that you possess inside.
You don't have to hide your feelings that you hold deep inside.

Let your mind run free
Let me help your reach that point of ecstasy.

Allow me to make your womanhood
Rise to heights higher than the Himalaya Mountains.

Open your heart and let me run free.
Let me coat each inch of your heart with my love.

LOVE?

Can I truly say
That I am in love with you?
Or am I just fascinated
With the desire of being in your arms?

Being held all night long,
You kissing me while singing a sweet song.

Can I truly say
That I am in love with you?

I get mesmerized by looking at you;
I get so confused I know not what to do.

Can I truly say
That I am in love with you?

Everything that we have done together
Can be done once over again,
But how many times must we go through it
In order for me to say "I'll do it."

I'll spit out those words
Which so many men fear;
Those three simple words
In which you hold dear.

I can't say, "I love you"
'Cause I know not what love is,
But if it is anything like you,

My dear,
I'll run to it
With open arms and no fear.

LOVE ETERNAL

As I kiss the palm of your hand,
You hold my love.
As I kiss your forehead,
You hold our memories.
As I kiss your lips,
You hold a treasure untold.

Just your smile brings a
Glow about my face.
In your presence, my heart
Begins to race.

When I look into your eyes
I become stunned by your beauty,
Entering into an endless cycle of
Beautiful dreams and fantasies.

Your love is something so sweet and special to me.
I have the passion to love you for an eternity.
My love is like a waterfall,
Endlessly flowing into the depths of eternity.

Not even space or time could contain the
Love I have for you.
It would take a million lifetimes just to bring
My heart back down to reality.

If this is a dream,
Don't wake me,
'Cause I am in love with you.

LOVE PSALM

Looking through this glass window
I see things I've never seen before.
My love for you grows stronger even more.

Just by the touch of your hand
You mesmerize me with the sensations
You send through my body,
Caressing my heart in places
I thought never existed.

By your soft gentle breath
Breathing upon my skin,
My mind falls deeply into a trance
Thinking about our romance
And how we could take it to another level.

Your voice is so sweet
My heart yearns just to hear your voice.
Your words are so soft and mellow
You melt my heart every time you speak.

I can only imagine
What it would be like
Holding your hand in paradise.

But until that day
When I will see you face to face
And walk in the fullness of your grace . . .

Continue to caress my inner soul
Making me feel complete and whole.

MAN WITHOUT WOMAN

A man can't live without a woman.
A man without a woman
Is like unto a butterfly without any colors.
He is as unto an empty vessel,
Waiting to be filled.
Filled with that divine wine we call love.

Man can't live on bread alone.
He must take part of that wine to quench his thirst,
So that he may never thirst again.

A man's heart is like unto the midnight sky.
His heart is shallow, bitter and yet so cold.
The stars represent the holes in the heart of man.
When that fine, divine wine comes to fill his heart,
It leaks out like a waterfall.

Tell me what woman can pour her divine wine into my heart,
Making it overflow with eternal love.

MESMERIZED

I looked into her beautiful brown eyes,
And then I realized.
She has me mesmerized.
It's not because of her sexy hips,
Or her honey tasting lips.
It's because of her beauty,
Inside and out.

I stared into her eyes,
And saw the passion she had for me.
It was being locked up for an eternity.

I try to unlock that total mystery,
But trying to figure her out is like
Figuring out chemistry.

Why this doesn't come to my surprise,
It's because she has me mesmerized.

MOTION OF STILLNESS

I have just experienced beauty
Beyond my wildest imagination;
Beauty that can't be explained
With mere words,

Precious like a gemstone
Sparkling by the rays of moonlight.

This beauty I have discovered,
My mind can't comprehend this image.
It is sweet to my spirit and
Soothing to my soul.

To be able to hold and embrace this beauty
My heart was set at ease;
My heart rests and is at perfect peace
As the waters moved in a motion of stillness
And the sun rising, reflecting its
Beautiful rays upon the surface of the still river waters,
My soul is calm and at peace.

As I see the sparkle in your eyes
My inner spirit sings songs
As birds in the morning,

Rejoicing and singing praise to God
For placing a woman such as you in my life.

My mind is at ease,
My heart is at rest.
I ask myself, "Are you the one?"
Because this is too good to be true;

To have a woman whom
No man's eyes can contain her beauty,
I feel blessed beyond blessed.

MY DREAMS, VISIONS, AND HALLUCINATIONS

I have dreams
Of beautiful streams
Flowing with eternal love for each other.

I have visions
Of making that decision
Of living in your arms for an eternity.

I have hallucinations
About our destination
In this ever-long-lasting relationship.

I sometimes can't help but Let my mind wander,
Thinking about spending countless days
In paradise with you.

I can see myself
Massaging your feet
While feeding you something to eat.

I can envision myself
Tracing pathways on your back
With some ice,
Making you feel so nice.

I want to
Travel to distant lands
Just to walk hand in hand
On jet black sand.

But I can only do that
If I am your man,
Standing by your side
Holding your hand.

MY QUEEN

To God I give
The honor and the glory
For creating her.

For she is an
Image of beauty beyond
A man's comprehension.

To be with her
Is to be in heavenly
Places.

To touch her
Is to feel the soft gentle breeze
That God sends through.

To hear her voice
Is to hear the sweet sounds
Of birds singing.

To see her
Is like watching roses
Bloom in the spring.

She is as beautiful
As Gods nature.
Beside her I stand
And share my throne.

She is my Queen
She is my Wife.

MYSTICAL DESIRE

I can't explain
The reason why I love you.
It's like magic.

A mystical force placed a
Ring of fire around my heart.
Giving me a burning desire
To be a part of your life.

To hold you,
To kiss you,
To miss you.

For some reason
You make me complete.
For I was an entity
Separated from its other half.

I've searched greatly and stumbled upon you
And at that instant I knew,
It was real what I felt.
And for this reason,
I will never let you go.

I will walk the desert lands
Just to hold your hand.
I will cross any ocean or sea
Just for you to gaze at me.

The feeling of your presence is indescribable.
No man on earth can comprehend what I feel.

Allow me to take your hand
And show you worlds only dreamed of.
Let me open the doors to your fantasies
So I can fulfill your every desire.

Let this burning desire within my heart
Quench your thirst for love.
Allow this burning inferno to absorb and engulf
Your heart with a passion of love
That is indescribable.

PRECIOUS

You are beautiful to me,
Precious as gems.
Diamonds, emeralds and pearls
Have nothing on the beauty you possess.

To me, you shine inward and out,
Sparkling like twilight,
Shinning like moonlight.

As the dewdrops
Rest on the petals of gentle roses
I close my eyes and dream,
Hoping to catch your presence in my sleep;
Hoping to catch some beauty
That can compare to yours.

SIMPLE THOUGHTS

Can I gaze into your eyes
Spending a lifetime roaming
Fields of fantasies with you?

Can I rest my head upon your chest
Allowing my heart to come to a rest
Ending its long journey searching
For that eternal love?

I just want to spend some time
Rubbing your feet,
Feeding you things to eat.

Strawberries and Champaign,
Taking showers in the rain.
How beautiful are they,
And with thee
Beautiful shall it ever be.

SMILE

I want you to smile
For nothing on this earth can compare.

I see the twinkling stars in the sky;
It reminds me of the sparkle in your eyes.
I see the moon shine its bright rays on the river at night;
It reminds me of the flowing beauty that you possess.

Let me not hold back these feelings!
Let me not hold this overflowing river of Love!

Don't try to build up a wall
Blocking off the flow of my love;
Take a dip in my river and get wet.

Let my love not only moisten the surface of your heart,
But fill your vessel and let it over flow with eternal love.

THE QUESTION

Like moonlight licking
An ocean's naked waves,
I want to give you pleasure
Until my dying days

I want to quench
Your desire that burns like fire
Discovering all your fantasies,
Bringing them into reality

Allow me to kiss your lips a thousand times,
As you lay back and ease your mind.

Let me take you to a place
Where we would share pleasure
Without any disgrace.

I want to look into your eyes
And lose track of time,
Forgetting about our worldly needs
Just thinking about our fantasies

All my life I've been waiting for someone like you;
You leave no doubt in my mind that your love is true.

Let me get on one knee
And look up to thee
Asking but one question:

Will you marry me?

THESE FEELINGS

I never kissed you,
And yet I miss you.
I never held you,
And yet I want to tell you:
How much I want to hold,
How much I want to caress,
How much I want to lay my head on your chest.

I love you,
And yet I don't know you.
This is strange,
But is it possible this was temptation
That turned into an infatuation
Which resulted in the satisfaction
Of our inner desires?

I heard a song,
"I want to get next to you."
It's true when they said,
I want to get next to you.
Reason why?
So I can hold you
Mold you,
Kiss you,
Miss you,
Caress you,
Embrace you,
Letting you know that I care
And am willing to share
This love I feel so deep inside.
I don't want to hide these feelings,
So I will allow my feelings to give you
A sensual healing.
Letting you feel the deep passionate love
That I have for you.

THIRST FOR LOVE

If you thirst for love,
I ask that you
Take a gentle thorn
And prick my heart and draw blood.

Take your cup and fill it;
Fill it with the flow of my love.
Take your lips and drink
Until you can't drink any more.

If you ever thirst for love,
Take your cup and drink
From the fountain of my pricked heart.

It flows with an ever-flowing
Stream of love,
Waiting for you to drink
And never thirst again.

TOTAL ECLIPSE

Let my love orbit your world,
Creating a total eclipse of love,
Foreshadowing those things to come.

Let me whisper sweet words in your ear,
Making you feel like you're the only thing
That matters under the sun.

Let me kiss you on your collarbone,
Sending a sweet chilling sensation
Throughout your body.

As the candles burn,
Let our bodies twist and turn,
Giving each other total pleasure
Beyond our wildest imagination.

Let our bodies merge into one,
Until we discover our most intimate fantasies.

Let me nibble here and there,
Until I find your spots of ecstasy.

Let me caress your body
Until it is tender to my touch.

Chilling your body down with ice,
Let the candles burn out as I give you total pleasure.

Come let us fulfill each other's fantasies,
Leaving no part undiscovered.

TRUE ESSENCE

What is the true essence of a man?
What is the true essence of a woman?

For the two to join as one,
For one to complete the other.

What is the true essence of a man?
What is the true essence of a woman?

For a woman to take the man's hand,
Engage in a passionate relationship,
Fulfilling the dreams and fantasies
Only imagined and conceived with the
Deep part of the heart and mind.

I ask . . .
What is the true essence of a man?
What is the true essence of a woman?

Is it to walk to distant lands?
To give each other support to stand
And walk together as God's woman and man?

What is the true essence of a man?
What is the true essence of a woman?
Better yet . . .
What is the true essence of Love?

YOUR BEAUTY

The beauty you posses
No man can ever take
For God has blessed you
With a shade of caramel
And lips tasting like chocolate.

He blessed you with eyes that
Sparkle like diamonds,
And allowed you to speak
With the voice of angels.

He blessed you with a shape
That catches every man's eye,
Stunned with a glimpse
But mesmerized with a stare.

He blessed you with a fragrance
Compared to a field of roses.

Your intelligence
Goes beyond a man's comprehension.

So let me speak now
Or forever hold my peace:
You're beautiful in every way I mention
So allow me to focus my attention
On you and only you.

Blocking out everything
That surrounds me,
For you and me
It is bound to be destiny.

YOUR FRAGRANCE

Your fragrance
I can smell miles away.
Your smile,
I can see like a brighter day.
Your touch,
I can feel even in my sleep.

As I dream,
I see visions of love.
Visions of romantic nights.
Visions of playful fights.

I can see you and me
Living this life of love
For an eternity.

Spending endless hours
Taking hot steamy showers.
Walking on the beach
To watch the sunset within the sea.

I want to spend a lifetime
With you on my mind.

I want to be your ocean
And I want you to be my sand.

I want us to be together as one,
Knowing that God's great work
Has been done.

TEARS OF A MANN

When one loses Love
His soul becomes a vessel for pain;
Harnessing the remains of a broken heart.

What is strong enough to purge
A man's soul of this pain?

A NOVEL OF MYSTERY

I fell in love with a novel.
This was a novel of mystery.
Every day I gazed my eyes upon that novel and wondered ...
Can I unlock the mystery of this novel?
Can I discover the raveled secrets that lie between its most precious pages?
Can I for the first time, unravel and conquer a mystery on my own?

The belief and confidence in myself was so uncontrollable.
There have been many nights,
I fell asleep with this beautiful mystery.
Waking up looking at its most beautiful pages lying on my chest.
There have been so many nights I have thought about the conclusion of this mystery,
Being so eager to finish this lovely mystery.

But as I began to read deeper and deeper into this most precious novel,
I discovered some facts I couldn't make sense of.
I didn't want to give up, because it is not in my nature.
For it was truly in my heart to finish and complete this wonderful novel of mystery.

But as time had gone by,
I finally opened my eyes to realize,
There are not enough clues for me to conclude this wonderful novel
    of mystery.
Sometimes I feel as if this mystery doesn't want me to solve her.

Yet I am determined.
For I will close this mystery today,
Only to open it up another day.

For I need a little time away,
To get my thoughts together.
But I shall return to unravel
The mystery she so deeply contains.

Just remember one thing while I am away . . . .
I have always loved you,
From the bottom of my heart.
LaToya, I Love you.

AN EXPRESSION OF PAIN

I've searched to find someone
To replace the love that you give,
But their love gives me no reason
Why I should live.

I find myself closing my eyes,
Traveling back in time to where our love was strong,
Trying to figure out where our hearts went wrong.

The loneliness got me twisted,
And this tragedy has made me see
That you are the only one for me.

You say you need time,
I say I need you.
I can't stand by
And watch your love
Run away from my heart.

When I look at you,
I see my reflection,
So I offer my affection,
Love and dedication.

And I have come to realize,
There is no me, if there is no you.

CAN WE TALK?

Can we talk,
Just for a minute?
I have some things I must say
And these words I cannot delay.

You must realize
I've been hypnotized
By your beauty and
Stunned by your personality.
You've made my dreams
Turn into reality.

But you turned
And walked away,
Making my days
So dark and gray.

I can't explain
Through simple words
How much I miss you.
So I express them in the
Simple things that I do.

Sing to you
Sweet songs like I used to.
Buy you some Reese's
When I get the chance to.

I want to feed you
Strawberries and whip cream.
For this is my dream.

I want to be your "Pooh,"
But only if
You allow me to.

I want to kiss you,
But I am afraid I'm
Going to miss you.

Missing the late nights of
Holding you tight.
I don't want to
Put up a fight,
'Cause I know this is right.

I just need a chance
To show you love and romance.

I ask you,
Will you take that chance?

DAYS GO BY

Days go by
And yet I still have no one to hold.
I have no one to hold my lonely soul.
No one to caress,
No one to lay their head on my chest.

Some say its best
To lay down at night,
Holding your pillow tight,
Keeping up the fight,
Of that sensual healing.

But I have no doubt
That I must be about
That holding and molding,
That caring and sharing,
That chasing and embracing,
That kissing and missing.

See it's in my nature
That I must chase her.
To grab her
And claim her.
To say she is divine
And tastes like sweet wine.

But I dread
That her heart is dead
Therefore . . . .

Days go by
And yet I still have no one to hold.
I have no one to hold this lonely soul.
I still have no one to call my own.

EVERY TIME

Every time I look into your eyes,
I can't help but dwell on the memories locked up inside me.
Every time I hear your voice,
I can't help but think about the long conversations that we had.
Every time I feel the touch of your hand,
I can't help but think of the nights you fell asleep in my arms.

You meant everything to me.
You were my sunshine, during those rainy days.
You were my summer breeze, during those days of uncontrollable heat.
You were my comfort, during my times of stress.

I gave you my entire heart,
Leaving not a single piece behind for me.
My heart was a fragile vessel,
But it has been dropped,
Shattered into a thousand pieces.

I picked up the pieces,
Only to learn that loving you hurts.
Learning and coming to know that,
If I pick up the pieces and place them back in your hands,
They may fall and shatter once again.

I never realized that Love hurts,
And I have been hurt to many times before.
But like Edgar Allan Poe said, "NEVERMORE."

HEY BABE

Hey beautiful.
Hey tell me something.
Remember what we had?
Where did the love go?

Do you remember me holding you tight,
Just about every night?
Do you remember me staring into your eyes,
Getting lost in your eternal beauty?
Do you remember the nights when we would lie in each other's arms,
Looking forward to forever?
But, where did the love go?

There were times where I would look at you
And didn't even want to touch you.
The reason why, you ask?

To me you were like unto a precious gemstone,
Yet to be tarnished.
A perfectly cut diamond, sparkling like a golden nugget.
Like unto a butterfly, your personality flowed with many beautiful colors.
But, where did the love go?

Beauty, intelligence, and a beautiful smile.
What more could a man ask for?
You were a once-in-a-lifetime girl to me.
But tell me, where did the love go?

But Babe, I still got love for you.

I BLEW IT!

You worked so hard to gain her trust.
You worked so hard to gain her touch.
You finally get the chance to look into her eyes and see
The love that she possessed for thee.

But all that you have worked for,
All that you have built,
It all just crumbled in front of you.

How does it feel?
This question, it can't be real.

You feel as if the rug has just been snatched out from under you.
You feel as if someone stabbed you and left you to die.
You feel as if the one your life depended on has just been taken away
    from you.

Your world becomes a total disaster.
Everything around you crumbles at your feet.
You become dysfunctional throughout your daily life.

You can't eat.
You can't sleep.
You become so weak,
You can't even breathe.

How can this pain you feel be so real?
You spent a year of your life,
Wining and dining,
Caressing and embracing,
Holding her tight,
With all of your might.

And now,
What do you have to show,
For all that work you put in?

You lost all that you worked for,
Because you didn't want to open your eyes.
You didn't want to realize,
That what you have been asking for,
You already had.

You look for a title,
And yet you had that item all along.

Because of your ignorance,
You lost all that you built.
Because of your selfishness she is lost,
And maybe forever will she be out of your life.

I Blew it.
I Blew it with my ignorance.

LAST CHANCE

Listen,
You know the deal,
You know how I feel.

My love has always been true,
I've never let you down, Boo.

All I want is to express my love
Through terms never mentioned before.

All I want is to show my love
Through visions never dreamed before.

I want to walk down a path of love,
Never looking back at the pain and agony
Of my broken heart.

I want you to hold my heart in your hand
And seal it with your love.

For I can't walk down this path of love
Knowing you're not a part of me.

For your love reigns supreme;
There is nothing that could ever topple it.

You are my stars, my moon, and my night sky.
You are my tears of joy when I cry.

I want you to look into my eyes
And tell me where your heart lies.

For this is your last chance,
Be mine.

LOVE EXPERIENCE

Let me tell you about
A love experience that I had.
It was nice
Until it went bad.

It was nice and sweet
When it started.
But it just left me
Broken hearted.

I couldn't believe
She left me on my knees
Begging her please
Take me back so
My mind can rest at ease.

I felt used and abused
And I just refused
To open my eyes to realize
Her faults outweighed my needs
And it left me paralyzed and on my knees.

Many people saw the pain I felt,
And they offered to help,
But I turned my head in shame
For I didn't want them knowing my name

It wasn't right,
But I had to fight.
These feelings of being blue
For I knew this couldn't be true.

For I was feeling down and in the dump
And I had to get up and off this hump.
For I had come to understand
I am a man and I must stand.

My life wasn't over,
I had just begun
So I could walk down
That path once again.

SILENCE

I saw you the other day
Walking in your own little way.
I wanted to tell you
What I was thinking
But I became afraid.

Not because I was scared of you
But because I was scared of rejection.
The rejection of you not listening
To the words I had to say.

I was afraid you would
Close your ears
And shut your heart,
Causing me to talk and waste my time.

This is the reason why I choose to die,
Not literally,
But emotionally
Causing a scare in my heart
Deeper than any ocean and sea.

I've been hurt many times before
And I can't go through that pain any more.
So I kept my mouth shut,
Keeping my heart and feelings in silence.

TEARS OF A MANN

Is a man truly a man
If he don't cry?
Having tears drop
From each corner of his eye?

Each tear represents a memory;
A memory he held so very dear.

Memories of loving nights
And passionate desires
Turned into sleepless nights
And a dimmed fire.

Each tear falling from his eye
Causing pain from shattered dreams
And a broken heart;
The sweeter the memory
The deeper the pain.

Each tear that falls
Feels like a knife,
Making tiny incisions in his heart;
Causing pain beyond his wildest imagination,
Causing wounds that will take years to heal.

Being tortured by many
Restless nights
And beautiful dreams
Turned into lonesome nightmares.

Falling asleep in tears
Only to awaken in more tears.

But...
Is a man truly a man
If he don't cry?

TIRED

Tempting though it may be
It's a trap and
This I can clearly see

With your soft puffy lips
And your coke-bottle hips,
Flaunting them around me just for kicks.
Girl, I would be trapped in a hole six feet deep
And this is a challenge I am not willing to meet.

Being caught up in webs of illusions
Being tossed by mad winds of confusion.

Please!
Let me not even fool myself,
Getting caught up with you
Is like a bad hand being dealt.

I have no more love to give
And with you, I am not trying to live.
You crushed my heart once before
And now you come back for more?

Please,
I have no time.
I am trying to lay back and unwind
'Cause fooling with you,
I lost my everlasting mind!

THE QUESTION—THE ANSWER

I remember you posing a question
Not too long ago.
You asked me why I'm in your life.
The <u>why</u> I do not know.

I've listened to your voice tone
Your words so carefully slow
At this time the answer to your question
I still do not know.

I see life as being a puzzle
And it sometimes boggles the mind
But there are clues that we must follow
If the answers we are to find.

A jig-saw makes a picture
With pieces that fit here and there.
They do not always fit where we may think
But like the pieces of a puzzle
I fit in your life somewhere.

Life has its mountains and valleys
And waters that sometimes flow.
Where in your life do I fit?
The answer I do not know.

If I could choose to be part of a day
I'd be a summer's breeze,
To bring relief from the hot sunshine
And the wish that I would not leave.

Or maybe I'd be the evening sun
As it begins to set,
To bring a peaceful view of shadows and colors
As the horizon it has met.

Or maybe I'd be the waters that caress the sandy beach,
The pleasant waves that come and gently go.
But where in your life I will find my place
I really do not know.

I am a part of your picture,
Which part I cannot say,
But once the picture is complete,
Please do not throw my part away.

I remember you posing a question
Not too long ago.
You asked me why I'm in your life.
The <u>why</u> I do not know.

I wonder sometimes myself.

A WALK IN THE SPIRIT

To gain Godly Wisdom
You must first lose your own wisdom.

To gain Godly understanding
You must first lose your own understanding.

To gain Godly righteousness
You must first lose your own righteousness.

To gain Godly love
You must first lose your own love.

The life of lovers is in death
For one cannot win the heart of God
Unless he first lose his own.

A BATTLE

I am fighting a battle deep within
Whether to turn around and do good
Or keep my hand in this bag of sin.

Deep down inside I know what is right
But every time I am faced with the same fight,
The fight of temptation.

The fight of lusting for the opposite sex.
The need for her soft hands caressing my head,
The thoughts and wonders of her lying in my bed.

I have yet to overcome this weakness
Because I do nothing to make myself stronger.

I sit here and wonder what to do
But I know the first step,
I know the rules.

I must make up in my mind
Which hands will deal my cards.
Will it be the hands of goodness?
Or will it be the hands of evil?

The hands of evil give me all that I want
But the hands of goodness will give me what I need.

For there is a price that comes with the things I want
But I have never considered the things I needed.

I must choose carefully when playing with these cards.
'Cause if I don't . . . .
I am fighting a battle deep within . . . .

A MESSAGE

Once again I feel the pain
Of my lonely heart.

The jealousy of seeing others in love.
My heart craves for the touch of a woman.
And yet my heart must feel the pain of withdrawal.
For I am taking a new path in life.

I must purify myself of this crazy mindset,
Believing that I need to be with a woman,
Believing that her touch would solve all my problems.
Not realizing that she was the cause of my problems all along.

I blocked my vision with these women,
Never having the chance to see what God had in his plan.
By the taste of that lustful wine,
I've crossed that line of temptation and became
Infatuated by the shapes of these beautiful creatures.
They dazzled me with the swaying of their hips.
They mesmerized me with the fullness of their lips.

Many shapes and sizes,
Intelligence to no elegance,
They hypnotized me and kept my mind lost in a mist of darkness,
Running farther away from the light,
Never getting the chance to see what is right.

With the soft touch of their hands
They sent me on a cruise sailing the seven deadly seas,
Having the chance to dip and indulge myself into each sea of sin.
I've became blind and lost track of time.
My mind was thrown in a loop,
Never given the chance to escape this torture.

To all men, heed my warning:
"Flee from the strange woman
For the lips of a strange woman drop as an honeycomb,
And her mouth is smoother than oil;"
"Her house is the way to hell, going down to the chambers of death."

(Proverbs 5:3; 7:27)

A SIMPLE FAVOR

To take my place,
You can't face,
The pain and agony.
The discomfort and disrespect,
You couldn't take it.

I was placed on a cross
To save you from sin
And you turn around
And say I'm not kin.

Deep within
You say you love me,
But by you not showing it
You draw far from me
Each and every day.

I ask you to do simple things
But you turn your back and
Ignore the words I speak.
I ask you to read my bible
Just once a day or even once a week
But you refuse and say, "I'm too busy."

You know,
I know you never thought of it this way,
But what if you ask me
To write your name in my "Book of Life"
But I refuse and say,
"I'm too busy."
That wouldn't be right,
But isn't that the same?

You ask me to do a simple favor
And I refuse and say,
"I'm too busy."

I made the ultimate sacrifice
And you can't do me a simple favor.
Now I can see how much
You truly love me.

Your heart is cold and dark
As a stormy winter night.

It isn't right
That I give up my life
And you can't do me a simple favor.

Well maybe I'll just forget to
Write your name in my "Book of Life."
Maybe then will you see me
As your savior
And do me that simple favor.

A TALK WITH SATAN

Satan, you know what I want.
You know my weakness
But you fail to realize that I am
Determined not to fall.

Because of the grace of God
I have seen the light
And by his power and might
I now know what is right.

I can stand tall
And look down on you
Knowing that you are small.

You can't put up a brick wall
To try to make me fall.
You can't stop my acceleration in God
Because I set no limitations
On my constant meditations.

A lot of people see you as a big problem;
Even a big issue.
You're nothing more than a small condition
And with my decision
You have no other choice but to move
When I make mention.

For I have the power
That Jesus had in the day
And with that power
He shows me the way

Truth and righteousness is now my path
So I may never see God's wrath.

AFTER THE STORM

When everything goes wrong,
Remember, there's a blessing
After the Storm.

When everything goes from perfect communication
To dysfunction and total corruption,
Remember, there's a blessing
After the Storm.

You're feeling stress
And your life's a mess,
But remember, there's a blessing
After the Storm.

God tends to paint a picture for you throughout your life.
He allows you to see only parts of the picture that he paints
Because you wouldn't be able to handle the whole blessing all at once.

So as you go through your trials and tribulations,
It is your obligation to remember always
There's a blessing
After the Storm.

ASHAMED

Once again I come before your face,
Down on my knees asking for your grace.
I feel like a total disgrace,
Now wishing if someone else could take my place.

I ask myself,
"Do I deserve this peace which you give me?"

I've turned my back against your face,
Knowing I needed your grace.
I looked into my heart and saw
The darkness, the deceit, and the lust for all the
Unrighteousness you've tried to keep me from,
But now I see what I have become.

I was enticed by the darkness
And stepped over that line.
It was only a matter of time
Until I lusted after the sin the darkness offered.

It led me down dark roads,
Never knowing its end,
Stumbling over things I could not see,
I felt the pain and so much misery,
But you see it didn't bother me.
'Cause I was on top of the world,
Even though Satan had a hold on my soul.

I tried to be bold and take it back,
But Satan smiled and laughed at that.
He said, "I am not giving it back without a fight,
So you better come at me with a bigger bite."

So I fell to my knees and asked God for some might.
Then he held me back and said,
"Son this is no longer your fight, but mine."

Remember: The battle is not yours, but the Lord's.

COMFORTER

From day in to day out
You continue to fight
Just to see a little bit of light.

You're tired and can't go on.
Your storms become a little too strong,
While everything else turn up so wrong.

You've counted up the cost
And found out that all is lost;
You feel all alone with no way home.
You're trapped in a world of confusions,
Twisted up by so many illusions.

Understand God's master plan And you will be able to stand. Just take
    his hand and
He will guide you to that promised land.

God will send his Comforter to be a light
Piercing through the darkness to
Guide you through the night.

Remember he sent his Comforter
To be your peace and strength
Which will help you endure to the end.

Now I ask you, "Do you need my friend, the Comforter?"

CURIOSITY

He designed a plan
And now I understand.
He uses your curiosity to lure you in,
Causing your imagination to do the sin.

Your Curiosity is the key.

It gets you enticed to the point where you ponder.
It makes you feel nice, while your mind tends to wander.

It wanders off with your imagination.

You began to imagine
Things never dreamed before;
Things never seen before.
After a while you become that whore.

Doing things you said you wouldn't do;
Doing things you told others they shouldn't do.

Let me explain why you fell in this whole of sin:

Your curiosity is the key
To unlock that mystery of your memory.
It triggers your imagination,
Causing you to yield to all sorts of temptation.

If you control your curiosity
You can control your temptation.
If you can't control your curiosity
It will lead you straight to damnation.

EXAMINATION OF MYSELF

I ask myself
Is there anything else to be felt?
I've done dwelt
In the midst of evil,
Dwelt in a mist of confusion.
I must now walk away from this illusion,
Making sure it comes to a conclusion.

I must make the choice
To lift my voice
In the direction of perfection.

Not to be stalled
By any brick wall
That I may have to climb
Causing me to fall behind.

I must not stumble
Over any block
Causing me to fall
In my walk.

I want to see a brighter day
So I lift my hands and pray
That I may continue in His way.

I'm striving to stay alive
In the presence of the Lord's eyes,
And I've come to realize
There is no surprise
When it comes to the Most High.

FOCUS

Let's put things into perspective:
What is your main objective?
What is the course set for your life?

You strayed away
And now you struggle
Day by day.

You got in too deep
Now you are so weak
You can barely speak.

You don't have that flame in your eyes anymore
You look at yourself and see a whore.

Where is the dedication to overcome this situation?
Wasn't that your primary obligation?

Meditation is an invitation
To define the situation
That you may have an obligation
To overcome without limitation.

So look forward with no hesitation
To correct the situation.

Now get your focus right!

HEAVY HEART

Confusion within the heart
Drives you apart,
From the things you need
And draws you closer to
The things you want.

Like a child,
I see some things I want
And become stubborn
In my ways,
Causing me to feel guilt
Throughout my days.

Even though I've been told
Not once,
Not twice,
But three times or more,
I still walk through that same door.

That door of temptation.
A door that I always face
And once I walk through,
I feel like a disgrace.

Sometimes I wonder.
Am I that weak,
That I fall to my knees
And can't stand on my own two feet?

I look at my past
And can't help but laugh.
But then I think,
How did I take the wrong path?

For I have been taught
The consequences of yielding to temptation.
And today I face the worst of them all:

A heavy heart.

HOW?

How can I refuse you?
How can I abuse you?
How can I turn my head and speak words of hatred to you?

You've done more for me than anyone in history.
You told me you loved me and showed it,
Even when I would curse you and spit in your face.
I ask you, how can you love someone like me?

I don't understand you.
Explain to me, how can you love me?
The one who laughs in your face when you
Spoke nothing but encouraging words to me.
The one who was ashamed to mention your name in public.
The one who would not listen even in life-threatening situations.

Tell me how can you do it?
Every day you are called out by your name more than a thousand times,
And yet you sit there and act as if it doesn't even bother you.

This just doesn't add up.
Please,
Explain this to me, 'cause this brother just don't understand.
How can you take all this and yet still love me?

Answer . . .

Because I care,
For I am your father. For I am the Lord.

IT'S YOURS TO CONTROL

Expecting the expected
But instead you receive the unexpected
Your efforts neglected
And your beliefs not respected.

When you strive for the best
But instead you receive less
And think you're not blessed
And overcome with stress;
Now comes the test.

Weather you will give up the fight
Or stay in the dark until you see light
Or stay in the storm
Whether you will sulk in sorrow
Or live for tomorrow.

Seeing, believing, you can still achieve
Your dream and what you first believed
And knowing you will eventually receive.

Your dream and goal, are determined by
Your aspiration, dedication and determination
Without hesitation and constant meditation
For your destiny is in your hand and at your command
On these words meditate and understand.

MY LORD SPEAKS

I chose you to do my work
But you refused and closed my book.
You turned your head from my ways
To live in the mist of confusion
For the rest of your days.

I don't understand
Why you took this path.
All I wanted was
For you not to see my wrath.

You chose to be disobedient.
You chose to live unpleasant.
I'll give you one more chance.
Don't spoil it by doing your own dance.

Repent and be born again
And I promise you I'll wipe away all your sins.
You will be clean and set free
To walk and talk just like me.

Don't mess up and go astray
'Cause then will I turn my back and walk away.

So don't blow this chance
And do your own dance
'Cause I will walk away
Not thinking of you another day.

MY UNDERSTANDING

Many years I've wanted love.
Many years I've received less than what I gave.
But I didn't realize I was giving it
To the wrong person.

I've came to the understanding
That love is very demanding,
Giving my heart and soul
Never knowing the feelings that my other may hold.

I realized I've been giving my love to the wrong one,
Even though I thought it was all said and done.
I gave my love to a woman
And not to the Creator of that woman.

I allowed my imagination to run wild,
Causing my determination for goals to get mild.

My situation became stronger
And I couldn't step to it no longer.

My situation overrode my determination
And through my observation
I set up all kinds of limitations.

Through my hesitation
I didn't make it my obligation
To give God my situation.

But now I must not hesitate to meditate
So I may understand what God has in his plan,
So I may see beyond my natural eye,
That I may experiences things with my spiritual eye.

I want to become like Christ
And I must stand and take this fight
Just so I can do what is right.

"I'd rather live right, then live in Hell and lift up my eyes."

PERSPECTIVE

Let's put things back into perspective,
Cause quite frankly you've lost your objective.

You no longer know how to act
Because you are off track
And you know it's a fact.

Turn your life around,
Seek for higher ground.
Look into the light,
Fight with all your might,
Just to do that which is right.

You do that,
You will never fall short of a blessing.

Now if you don't hesitate
To meditate in God's word
Your problems and situations shall be resolved.
Surely this you must have heard.

You will find through your observation
That God makes no hesitation
To resolve your situation.

He sets no limitation
When he makes it his obligation.

Open your heart and mind to understand
That it is all in his hand.
And to see Gods beautiful master plan,
You must first take a stand
And hold on to his unchanging hand.

RAZOR SHARP IMAGINATION

Razor sharp is my imagination,
Cutting through my every thought of determination,
Turning the cold heart of a warrior
Into a warm passionate heart of a mother.

Lusting for those things I cannot touch,
Taunting my every silent moment with questions:

"What if?"
"What if I was to say …"
"What if I was to do …"

No!
This endless cycle must stop.
I can no longer be controlled by the desires of my eye.

I see her beauty,
I hear the sweet sounds of her voice
But …

I must remember my promise
I will wait on Him …

Until then,
I shall endure this pain
Of my "Razor Sharp Imagination."

REALIZATION

Once again
I got too close
And now I feel the
Pain of losing your
Sensual touch.

I look into your eyes
And I feel the agony
Of holding you in my arms.

I feel the pain
Of missing your sweet kisses;
So soft and gentle were they.

I tend to reminisce
Looking at you sleep,
As I listen to the soft
Sounds of you breathing.

I sometimes play back in my mind,
The nights we spent giving
Each other total pleasure.

But there has been a change
In my life,
Now I must strive to do right.

I've been summoned by a higher power
To uphold and keep a standard.

I can no longer put up a fight
I must turn around and live right.

I apologize if I ever hurt you.
But I want you to know,
I never meant to.

Your beautiful smile
Kept me in denial
Of the physical, mental and emotional attraction
That I had for you.

The attraction was so strong,
Even though I knew it was wrong.

But now I must face my destiny
And walk this path of righteousness.

But always remember
When I kiss you,
Deep down inside,
I miss you.

REFLECTION

Through my trials and tribulations
I have made an important observation:
That it's only in my dedication to Jesus
That I will ever overcome my situation.

The lust for Love.

Searching for a vessel of love
To fill this empty void
I've become mesmerized by the
Enchanting taste of that lustful wine.

Seeing visions of beautiful women
Touching the depths of my heart
Caressing my inner soul
Making me blind to the sin
That I do deep within.

From the look of a woman, I became hypnotized.
From the touch of a woman, I became mesmerized.
I fell into a world of confusion
Walking through a mist of illusions.

I tried to deal with the fallacy of this enticing reality
But I find there is no truth to these visions I see.
I find there is no truth to this deep dark reality.

So I have made the decision
That these illusions and this confusion
Must come to a conclusion.

For if I surrender my soul to sin
I'll never get the chance to see
That good that lies deep within.

THE CHOICE

All right let's face reality.
You planed out your life,
You figured out what's wrong and what's right.
He told you to choose
Between the dark and the light
So you hardened your heart
And chose the dark.

You chose to step foot
Into that lifestyle of temptations,
That led to your infatuations,
Leading up to all your altercations.

You chose that lifestyle of mortality
That has no morality.
You chose to keep that lifestyle of pain,
Leaving you with a deep, dark stain.

Now is the time
That you make up your mind.
Open your eyes and realize
That this lifestyle is not mild.
Come back to the light.
For **God** will bless you 'til all is right.

THE ROADS OF LIFE

Taking time out to think about life,
The wrongs and rights,
The pain and strife,
I have finally wakened up to see the shimmering light.

Life is as a road with many a turn,
Not knowing what way it will go,
And what out of it I will earn.

But I've learned
To live life day by day,
Letting the road I travel take me where it may.
And I pray,
That I will eventually find the right way.

But until I find the true and righteous path,
I pray the Lord will spare his wrath.
Until I'm in his loving arms at last.

D.B. '98
(Darryl E. Bethea)
3-26-98

TOTAL UNDERSTANDING

I know my purpose,
I know my reason for living,
And yet I refuse to open my eyes
To see the things He has prepared for me.

I see the things I want to see
And I try to be those things I want to be,
But I'll never be able to
Unlock the doors that are closed,
I'll never be able to
Move mountains that are too hard to climb;

I'll never be able to
Reach the stars in the night sky
Until I decide to let
The Lord use my mind and eyes;
Until I decide to let
The Lord use my heart, body and soul,
To do what has been told.

I will never be able
To see the solutions to my problems at hand;
Never will I be able to make a stand
Until I come to understand
I must let God use me totally.

WHAT TYPE OF LOVE IS THIS?

The love that you give
Goes beyond all knowledge.
It goes beyond anything that I've ever known.
It goes beyond my own comprehension.

They say that love is given to
Satisfy the hunger and thirst
Of physical, emotional, and mental completion,
But tell me how,
How can you love
Someone like me?

It would take more than a lifetime
For me to embrace the love you give.
This love is no ordinary love.
This is that unconditional love.
It's that type of love that purifies the hearts of man,
Leaving no evil thoughts or deeds inside.
It's that type of love that washes away all sins.
It's that type of love that makes you jump for joy.

What type of love is this,
That you would bear all my problems,
All my troubles,
All my sickness,
All my pain?
What type of love is this?

You open my eyes to see
My wrongs from my rights,
My struggles and my strife,
Then you show me it will be all right
Because it has already been worked out.

Just tell me what type of love is this.
No other love can ever come close
To the love you give me.
It would take a fool to let this kind of love go.
So tell me, what type of love is this?

WHO'S ARMY

Yeah you say you're a solider,
But in whose army?
The Lord's army or Satan's army?
You tell me.

Now look here,
You say you're in the Lord's army,
Then what's up with you?
You skip church.
You don't associate yourself with those who lift your spirits.
You look at them as if they are complete strangers.
You claim you don't feel comfortable in church any more.
Now you tell me,
What's the matter with you?

You used to be strong-minded.
Now every little thing influences you.
You used to be worry-free.
Now every little thing bothers you.
You used to never give up.
Now you give up in the blink of an eye.

God said, "Seek ye first the kingdom of Heaven, and all things will
Be added unto you."
So what is the problem?
You sought and found.
Why haven't you committed yourself like you're supposed to?

Think about it.
It's not what you want,
Its what He wants.
What God wants.

You claim you are a soldier in his army.
Then act like it!

He prepares his soldier the way He wants.
Preparing, them for the future,
For the future war.

You have to accept what you are going through.
It is only to better you.
Your trials,
Your tribulations,
They are all tests and exams.

Do you plan to fail,
Or do you plan to pass?

The choice to study is up to you. But tell me now,
Whose army are you in?

WHY?

They say we are nothing.
They say we are nobodies.
They tease us,
They pick at us,
They look at us with that look of destruction.
We ask them every day, "Why must you do these things to us?"

They reply . . . .
"Because you are not one of us. You are a child of God. Until you turn your face away from God, we will continue to tease you, pick at you every chance we get, give you that look of destruction, do those things that are ungodly in your face, and chastise you in every way. We will continue to do these things to you until you decide to become one of us."

I ask you why would you choose death rather than life?
Choose discomfort rather than comfort?
Choose displeasure rather than pleasure?
Satan over God?

If you choose temptation, lust, evil, you choose death (Satan).
If you choose love, comfort, satisfaction, you choose life (God). The choice is yours, my children.

Choose wisely my children, choose wisely.

WONDERING

You sit around wondering,
When will it be my turn?
When will it be my turn
To take part of that everlasting love?
When will it be my turn
To have someone by my side to love me for life?

You sit there staring off into the mist
Wondering and wishing for
Someone to love,
Someone to hold,
Someone to kiss,
Someone to miss
When you are far away,
Or in a moment of despair.

To be loved,
Oh what a feeling.
But wait . . .

You sit around wondering,
While the answer lies right in front of you.
All you have to do is open your eyes.
Realize all you have to do is reach out and grab it.
That eternal love you seek
Has been there since the beginning of time,
For it's the Lord.
He is that Eternal Love.

YOUR CHOICE

You have been away for so long.
Now you don't know right from wrong.
Everything you used to do becomes a struggle for you.
To stand and testify, you claim that you're very shy.
To kneel and pray, it would probably take you a day.
To stand and clap your hands you say, "It's a test to see if you're a man."

Things have changed.
No matter which way you see them.
Your heart has become cold and bitter
To the one who gave you life,
To the one who got rid of your troubles and strife.

Open your eyes and realize all He wants to do is love you,
Give you all that you need,
Quench that burning fire of your inner desires,
Take away your fears, and dry up all your tears,
Take away your pain and sorrow and show you tomorrow.

But the choice is yours,
Whether to push or pull,
Whether to walk or run,
Whether to look into the light or put up a fight.

Remember, the choice is yours.
But don't choose the wrong path and feel the lords' deadly wrath.

ABOUT THE AUTHOR

Daniel E. Bethea, Jr. hails from the Greater Capitol Heights region of Prince Georges County, Maryland. Born and raised by God fearing parents, their teachings spawned his devotion to helping people, and became central to his overall mission in life: To motivate and inspire greatness in others. As Daniel continues his journey in life, he relies on his faith in God and his determination for success, to reach the hearts and minds of people. Daniel's goal is to encourage and get the best out of everyone he encounters.

www.ingramcontent.com/pod-product-compliance
Lightning Source LLC
Chambersburg PA
CBHW070928160426
43193CB00011B/1605